If You Love Me
KEEP

MY

COMMANDMENTS

If You Love Me Keep My Commandments. Copyright © 2015 C. Orville McLeish. All rights reserved.

No rights claimed for public domain material, all rights reserved. No parts of this publication may be reproduced, stored in any retrieval system, or transmitted in any form or by any means, electronic, mechanical, recording, or otherwise, without the prior written permission of the author. Violations may be subject to civil or criminal penalties.

ISBN: 978-1-953759-19-1 (paperback)
ISBN: 978-1-953759-20-7 (hardback)
ISBN: 978-1-953759-21-4 (eBook)

Printed in United States of America

If You Love Me
KEEP
MY
COMMANDMENTS

COMPILATION OF COMMANDS ON CHRISTIAN LIVING AND ON WORSHIP

C. ORVILLE MCLEISH

Introduction

Jesus was asked in St. Mathew 22, "Teacher, which is the greatest commandment in the law?" he replied with two, "Love the Lord your God with all your heart and with all your soul and with all your mind. This is the first and greatest commandment. And the second is like it: Love your neighbour as yourself. All the Law and the Prophets hang on these two commandments." (St. Matthew 22:36-40)

The Christian community celebrated that Jesus reduced 613 commandments found in the Old Testament to only two under the New Covenant. As I meditated on this, I realized that we were missing something, and while loving God, and loving people may seem straightforward enough, it was not quite evident in the lifestyles of many Christians. While we get some part right, in other areas we were not doing so well. The Words of Jesus kept ringing in my spirit, "If you love me, you will keep my commandments." (St. John 14:15 - ESV)

The part I think we missed was, "All the law and prophets hang…"

I went on a personal retreat to revisit the New Testament and extract everything that would look like a command from Jesus. I numbered them as I went along and was very surprised to see that when this journey ended, the number was 613—the exact number of commands given in the Old Testament. I knew then that this book had to be released.

Within these pages you will find all the commands you will obey because of your love for Jesus. Every relationship is built on an understanding that there are the rules we abide by. Most of these things you will not, or cannot, do unless you have a genuine love for Jesus. While we know that the books of Matthew, Mark, Luke and John overlaps each other because it speaks to basically the same period of time, I did not seek to remove any duplicates. For example, "Fear not" "Do not be afraid" is a very common theme throughout, but I leave every instance it is given intact. I am still amazed that without removing any duplications or repeat of similar themes that the number would be 613.

I pray that as you read these verses, the love of God will explode in your heart and bring you even closer to his heart. he loves us perfectly, and unconditionally. It is our love for him that often comes into question.

As a bonus, I also included from the book of Psalms commands on Worship. Who better to influence our worship, and to learn from than the worshipper himself, King David!

This is a beautiful compilation that you will want to share with—well—everyone.

On Christian Living

1.
Let your light shine.
St. Matthew 5:16

2.
Do not be angry with your brother.
St. Matthew 5:22

3.
Do not insult your brother.
St. Matthew 5:22

4.
Do not call anyone fool.
St. Matthew 5:22

5.
Be reconciled to your brother before you present a gift to the Lord.
St. Matthew 5:24

6.
Do not look at a woman to desire her.
St. Matthew 5:28

7.

Do not divorce.

St. Matthew 5:32

8.

Do not marry a divorced woman.

St. Matthew 5:32

9.

Do not take oaths.

St. Matthew 5:34

10.

Your answer should be yes or no.

St. Matthew 5:37

11.

Do not resist an evildoer–turn the other cheek–go an extra mile–give more than ask for.

St. Matthew 5:39

12.

Give to the one who asks you. Do not reject the one who wants to borrow from you.

St. Matthew 5:42

13.

Love your enemies.

St. Matthew 5:44

14.
Pray for those who persecute you.
St. Matthew 5:45

15.
When you pray, go into your room, close the door and pray to the Father in secret.
St. Matthew 6:6

16.
When you pray, do not babble repetitiously.
St. Matthew 6:7

17.
Pray this way, "Our Father, who are in heaven. hallowed be your name. Thy Kingdom come. Thy will be done on earth as it is in heaven. give us this day our daily bread, and lead us not into temptation, but deliver us from evil. For thine is the kingdom. The power and the glory, forever."
St. Matthew 6:9-14

18.
Forgive others.
St. Matthew 6:14

19.
When you fast, put oil on your head and wash your face.
St. Matthew 6:17

20.

Do not accumulate treasures on earth.

St. Matthew 6:19

21.

Accumulate treasures in heaven.

St. Matthew 6:20

22.

You cannot serve God and money.

St. Matthew 6:24

23.

Do not worry about your life, what to eat, or what to wear.

St. Matthew 6:27

24.

Pursue his Kingdom and righteousness first.

St. Matthew 6:33

25.

Do not worry about tomorrow.

St. Matthew 6:34

26.

Do not judge.

St. Matthew 7:1

27.

Do not give what is holy to dogs or pigs.

St. Matthew 7:6

28.

Ask and receive; seek and find; knock and the door will be opened.

St. Matthew 7:7

29.

In everything treat others as you would want to be treated.

St. Matthew 7:12

30.

Enter through the narrow/difficult gate.

St. Matthew 7:13

31.

Show mercy, not sacrifice.

St. Matthew 9:13

32.

Let it be done to you according to your faith.

St. Matthew 9:29

33.

Teach, preach and heal like Jesus.

St. Matthew 9:35

34.

Use the authority God gives you.

St. Matthew 10:1

35.
Do not be afraid.
St. Matthew 10:26

36.
What Jesus tells you in the dark, say it in the light. What he tells you in secret, proclaim from the rooftops.
St. Matthew 10:27

37.
Do not fear the one who can just kill the body. Fear he who can destroy both soul and body in hell.
St. Matthew 10:26

38.
Acknowledge Jesus before men. Do not deny him.
St. Matthew 10:32

39.
Do not love father, mother, son or daughter more than Jesus.
St. Matthew 10:37-38

40.
Take up your cross and follow Jesus.
St. Matthew 10:38

41.
The kingdom suffers violence, the violent take it by force.
St. Matthew 11:13

42.

Come to Jesus all who are weary and burdened, and he will give you rest.

St. Matthew 11:28

43.

See Jesus as greater than the temple.

St. Matthew 12:6

44.

Pray for all sick to be healed.

St. Matthew 12:15

45.

Do not blaspheme the Holy Spirit (speak against).

St. Matthew 12:27-32

46.

Do not waste words.

St. Matthew 12:36-37

47.

Do not ask for a sign.

St. Matthew 12:39

48.

Repent when the gospel is preached.

St. Matthew 12:41

49.

Be filled with the Spirit.

St. Matthew 12:43-45

50.

Sow on good ground.

St. Matthew 13:8

51.

Listen to the Word.

St. Matthew 13:9

52.

Know the secrets of the kingdom.

St. Matthew 13:11-12

53.

Learn to see, listen and understand.

St. Matthew 13:13-14

54.

Open your eyes, ears and hearts.

St. Matthew 13:15-17

55.

The wheat must grow together with the tares until the great harvest.

St. Matthew 13:30

56.

Small seeds sown can become a great harvest.

St. Matthew 13:32

57.

Always speak the truth.

St. Matthew 14:4

58.

Feed the people.

St. Matthew 14:16

59.

Do not be afraid.

St. Matthew 14:27 (See also 17:7)

60.

Come.

St. Matthew 14:29

61.

Just believe.

St. Matthew 14:31 (See also 15:38)

62.

Honor your father and mother.

St. Matthew 15:4

63.
Be careful of the words you speak.
St. Matthew 15:11 (See also Verse 18)

64.
Guard your heart.
St. Matthew 15:19

65.
Have compassion.
St. Matthew 15:32

66.
Beware of the yeast of the Pharisees and Sadducees.
St. Matthew 16:6

67.
Whatever you bind on earth is bound in heaven.
St. Matthew 16:19

68.
Deny yourself, take up your cross and follow Jesus.
St. Matthew 16:24

69.
Have faith.
St. Matthew 17:20

70.

Fast and pray.

St. Matthew 17:21

71.

Pay your taxes.

St. Matthew 17:25-27

72.

Become like little children. Be humble like a little child.

St. Matthew 18:3 (See also 18:4)

73.

Welcome a child.

St. Matthew 18:5

74.

Do not cause children to sin.

St. Matthew 18:6

75.

Remove members of the body that cause you to sin.

St. Matthew 18:7-9

76.

Do not disdain a little child.

St. Matthew 18:10

77.

Always go searching for lost sheep.
St. Matthew 18:12-14

78.

Reveal your brother's fault in secret first.
St. Matthew 18:15-17

79.

Bind and loose
St. Matthew 18:18

80.

When two agrees, heaven responds.
St. Matthew 18:19

81.

Forgive your brother seventy- seven times from your heart.
St. Matthew 18:21 & 35

82.

Do not separate what God has joined.
St. Matthew 19:6 (See also 19:9)

83.

If you are able to accept the call of a Eunuch, accept it.
St. Matthew 19:12

84.
Always bless the children.
St. Matthew 19:14

85.
Do not murder.
St. Matthew 19:18-19

86.
Do not commit adultery.
St. Matthew 19:18-19

87.
Do not steal.
St. Matthew 19:18-19

88.
Do not give false testimony.
St. Matthew 19:18-19

89.
Honour your father and mother.
St. Matthew 19:18-19

90.
Love your neighbour as yourself.
St. Matthew 19:18-19

91.
Sell your possessions; give the money to the poor.
St. Matthew 19:21

92.
Follow Jesus.
St. Matthew 19:21

93.
Do not seek to be served, but serve.
St. Matthew 20:26-28

94.
No selling and buying in the temple.
St. Matthew 21:12

95.
Wear proper clothing.
St. Matthew 22:11-14

96.
Give to Caesar the things that are Caesar's, and to God the things that are God's.
St. Matthew 22:21

97.
Love the Lord your God with all your heart, with all your soul, and with all your mind.
St. Matthew 22:37

98.
Love your neighbour as yourself.
St. Matthew 22:39

99.
Practice what you preach.
St. Matthew 23:3

100.
Do not do good to be seen by people.
St. Matthew 23:5

101.
Call no one your 'father' on earth.
St. Matthew 23:9

102.
Do not allow yourself to be called a teacher.
St. Matthew 23:10

103.
Serve.
St. Matthew 23:11

104.
Humble yourselves.
St. Matthew 23:12

105.
Do not lock anyone out of the kingdom of heaven.
St. Matthew 23:13

106.
Do not neglect justice, mercy and faithfulness.
St. Matthew 23:23

107.
Do not be greedy or self-indulgent.
St. Matthew 23:25

108.
Watch out that no one deceives you.
St. Matthew 24:4

109.
Endure till the end.
St. Matthew 24:13

110.
Be ready.
St. Matthew 24:44

111.
Stay alert.
St. Matthew 24:42 (See also 25:13)

112.
Be like the wise virgins.
St. Matthew 25:1-13

113.
Use your talents to gain more.
St. Matthew 25:14-30

114.
Feed the hungry.
St. Matthew 25:35

115.
Feed the thirsty.
St. Matthew 25:35

116.
Be kind to strangers.
St. Matthew 25:35

117.
Cloth the naked.
St. Matthew 25:36

118.
Take care of the sick.
St. Matthew 25:36

119.

Visit those in prison.

St. Matthew 25:36

120.

Do not judge those who make great sacrifices.

St. Matthew 26:10

121.

Eat Jesus' body.

St. Matthew 26:26

122.

Drink Jesus' blood.

St. Matthew 26:27-28

123.

Stay awake and pray.

St. Matthew 26:41

124.

Do not respond to accusations.

St. Matthew 27:14

125.

Go and make disciples of all nations.

St. Matthew 28:19

126.
Baptize in the name of the Father and the Son and the Holy Spirit.
St. Matthew 28:19

127.
Teach them to obey my commands.
St. Matthew 28:20

128.
Repent and Believe the gospel.
St. Mark 1:15

129.
Follow me.
St. Mark 1:17 (See also 2:14)

130.
Have compassion.
St. Mark 1:41

131.
Put greater value on people, than on a day.
St. Mark 2:27

132.
Do not be afraid, just believe.
St. Mark 5:36

133.

Beware of the yeast of the Pharisees and Herod.

St. Mark 8:15

134.

Deny yourself, take up your cross and follow Jesus.

St. Mark 8:34

135.

If your hand causes you to sin, cut it off.

St. Mark 9:43

136.

If your foot causes you to sin, cut it off.

St. Mark 9:45

137.

If your eye causes you to sin, tear it out.

St. Mark 9:47

138.

Have salt in yourselves, and be at peace with each other.

St. Mark 9:49

139.

Let the little children come to Jesus.

St. Mark 10:14

140.
Have faith in God.
St. Mark 11:22

141.
Give to Caesar the things that are Caesar's and to God the things that are God's.
St. Mark 12:17

142.
Love the Lord your God with all your heart, with all your soul, with all your mind, and with all your strength.
St. Mark 12:30

143.
Love your neighbour as yourself.
St. Mark 12:31

144.
Watch out! Stay alert!
St. Mark 13:33 (See also Verse 37)

145.
Go into the world and preach the gospel to every creature.
St. Mark 16:16

146.
Do not live on bread alone.
St. Luke 4:4

147.
You are to worship the Lord your God and serve him only.
St. Luke 4:8

148.
You are not to put the Lord your God to the test.
St. Luke 4:12

149.
Do not be afraid.
St. Luke 5:27

150.
Follow Jesus.
St. Luke 5:27

151.
Love your enemies. Do good to those who hate you.
St. Luke 6:27

152.
Bless those who curse you. Pray for those who mistreat you.
St. Luke 6:28

153.
Turn the other cheek.
St. Luke 6:29

154.
Give to everyone who asks you.
St. Luke 6:30

155.
Do not ask for your possessions back from the person who takes them away.
St. Luke 6:30

156.
Treat others in the same way that you would want them to treat you.
St. Luke 6:31

157.
Love your enemies, and do good.
St. Luke 6:35

158.
Lend, expecting nothing back.
St. Luke 6:35

159.
Be merciful.
St. Luke 6:46

160.
Do not judge.
St. Luke 6:37

161.

Do not condemn.

St. Luke 6:37

162.

Forgive.

St. Luke 6:37

163.

Give.

St. Luke 6:38

164.

Deny yourself, take up your cross daily and follow Jesus.

St. Luke 9:23

165.

Go and proclaim the kingdom of God.

St. Luke 9:60

166.

Go!

St. Luke 10:3

167.

Whenever you enter a house, first say "May peace be on this house."

St. Luke 10:5

168.
Do not move around from house to house.
St. Luke 10:7

169.
Heal the sick and say, "The kingdom of God has come upon you."
St. Luke 10:9

170.
Rejoice that your names stand written in heaven.
St. Luke 10:20

171.
Be on guard against the yeast of the Pharisees, which is hypocrisy.
St. Luke 12:1

172.
Do not be afraid of those who can kill the body.
St. Luke 12:4

173.
Fear the one who has the authority to throw you into hell.
St. Luke 12:5

174.
Do not be afraid.
St. Luke 12:7

175.

Acknowledge me before men.

St. Luke 12:8

176.

Do not blaspheme the Holy Spirit.

St. Luke 12:10

177.

Watch out and guard yourself from all types of greed.

St. Luke 12:15

178.

Do not worry about your life.

St. Luke 12:22

179.

Pursue the kingdom of God.

St. Luke 12:31

180.

Sell your possessions and give to the poor.

St. Luke 12:33

181.

Get dressed for service, and keep your lamps burning.

St. Luke 12:35

182.
Be ready.
St. Luke 12:40

183.
Judge for yourself what is right.
St. Luke 12:57

184.
When you host an elaborate meal, invite the poor, the crippled, the lame, and the blind.
St. Luke 14:13

185.
No one can be Jesus' disciple if he does not renounce all his own possessions.
St. Luke 14:33

186.
Do not divorce and remarry.
St. Luke 16:18

187.
If your brother sins, rebuke him.
St. Luke 17:3

188.
If your brother repents, forgive him.
St. Luke 17:3

189.

Forgive.

St. Luke 17:4

190.

Always pray (persistently), don't lose heart.

St. Luke 18:1

191.

Let the little children come.

St. Luke 18:16

192.

Beware of the experts in the law.

St. Luke 20:46

193.

Watch out that you are not misled.

St. Luke 21:8

194.

Do not be afraid.

St. Luke 21:9

195.

Be on your guard.

St. Luke 21:34

196.
Stay alert at all times, praying.
St. Luke 21:35

197.
Pray that you will not fall into temptation.
St. Luke 22:40

198.
Do not make the Father's house a marketplace.
St. John 2:16

199.
Worship God in spirit and truth.
St. John 23-24

200.
Do not be afraid.
St. John 6:20

201.
Do not work for the food that disappears.
St. John 6:27

202.
Do not complain about Jesus to one another.
St. John 6:43

203.

Do not judge according to external appearance, but judge with proper judgment.

St. John 7:24

204.

Do not sin anymore.

St. John 8:11

205.

Practice the things you have heard from the Father.

St. John 8:38

206.

Do not love your life in this world.

St. John 12:25

207.

Believe in the light.

St. John 12:36

208.

Wash one another's feet.

St. John 13:14

209.

Love one another.

St. John 13:34 (See also 15:12)

210.
Do not let your hearts be distressed.
St. John 14:1

211.
Do not let your hearts be distressed or lack courage.
St. John 14:27

212.
Remain in me.
St. John 15:4

213.
Go and bear fruit.
St. John 15:16

214.
Feed my lambs. Shepherd my sheep. Feed my sheep.
St. John 21:15-17

215.
Follow me.
St. John 21:19

216.
Speak in new languages.
St. Mark 16:17

217.

Place your hands on the sick.

St. Mark 16:18

218.

When you receive holy Spirit, become a witness of Jesus to the world.

Acts 1:8

219.

What God has made clean, you must not consider ritually unclean.

Acts 10:15

220.

Abstain from meat that has been sacrificed to idols.

Acts 15:29

221.

Do not eat or drink blood from what has been strangled.

Acts 15:29

222.

Abstain from sexual immorality.

Acts 15:29

223.

Do not be afraid, but speak and do not be silent.

Acts 18:9

224.
It is better to give than to receive.
Acts 20:35

225.
Rejoice in sufferings.
Romans 5:3

226.
Do not let sin reign in your mortal bodies so that you obey its desires.
Romans 6:12

227.
Do not present your members to sin as instruments to be used for unrighteousness.
Romans 6:13

228.
Love without hypocrisy.
Romans 12:9

229.
Abhor what is evil, cling to what is good.
Romans 12:9

230.
Be devoted to one another with mutual love.
Romans 12:10

231.
Do not lag in zeal, be enthusiastic.
Romans 12:11

232.
Rejoice in hope.
Romans 12:12

233.
Endure in suffering.
Romans 12:12

234.
Persist in prayer.
Romans 12:12

235.
Contribute to the needs of the saints.
Romans 12:13

236.
Pursue hospitality.
Romans 12:13

237.
Bless those who persecute you.
Romans 12:14

238.
Rejoice with those who rejoice.
Romans 12:15

239.
Weep with those who weep.
Romans 12:15

240.
Live in harmony with one another.
Romans 12:16

241.
Do not haughty but associate with the lowly.
Romans 12:16

242.
Do not be conceited.
Romans 12:16

243.
Do not repay evil for evil.
Romans 12:21

244.
Live peaceably with all people.
Romans 12:18

245.

Do not avenge yourselves.

Romans 12:19

246.

Feed your enemies.

Romans 12:20

247.

Be subjected to the governing authorities.

Romans 13:1

248.

Pay everyone that is owed.

Romans 13:7

249.

Owe no one nothing, except to love them.

Romans 13:8

250.

Love your neighbour as yourself.

Romans 13:9

251.

Live decently at all times.

Romans 13:13

252.
Receive the one who is weak in faith.
Romans 14:1

253.
Do not have disputes over differing opinions.
Romans 14:1

254.
Do not pass judgement one another.
Romans 14:13

255.
Do not be a stumbling block to your sister or brother.
Romans 14:13

256.
Strong, bear with the failings of the weak, and do not seek to just please yourself.
Romans 15:1

257.
Agree together and end divisions and be united by the same mind and purpose.
1 Corinthians 1:10

258.
Do not judge anything before the time.
1 Corinthians 4:5

259.

Do not go beyond what is written.

1 Corinthians 4:6

260.

Do not associate with anyone who calls himself a Christian who is sexually immoral, or greedy, or an adulterer, or verbally abusive, or a drunkard, or a swindler.

1 Corinthians 5:11

261.

Flee sexual immorality.

1 Corinthians 6:18

262.

Married couples do not deprive each other of sex.

1 Corinthians 7:5

263.

Do not divorce.

1 Corinthians 7:11

264.

Keep God's Commandments.

1 Corinthians 7:19

265.

Do not become slaves of men.

1 Corinthians 7:23

266.

If you sin against your brother or your sister's weak conscience, you sin against Christ.

1 Corinthians 8:12

267.

Do not be adulterers.

1 Corinthians 10:17

268.

Do not be immoral.

1 Corinthians 10:8

269.

Do not put Christ to the test.

1 Corinthians 10:9

270.

Do not complain.

1 Corinthians 10:10

271.

Do not seek your own good.

1 Corinthians 10:24

272.

Eat everything that is old in the marketplace.

1 Corinthians 10:25

273.

Do everything for the glory of God.

1 Corinthians 10:31

274.

Do not give offense.

1 Corinthians 10:32

275.

Men, do not pray or prophesy with head covered.

1 Corinthians 11:4

276.

Women do not pray or prophesy with your head uncovered.

1 Corinthians 11:5, 10, 13

277.

Partake of the Lord's Supper.

1 Corinthians 11:23-28

278.

Do not be children in your thinking.

1 Corinthians 14:20

279.

Women should be silent in the churches.

1 Corinthians 14:34

280.

Do not forbid anyone to speak in tongues.

1 Corinthians 14:39

281.

Be firm. Do not be moved.

1 Corinthians 15:58

282.

Always be outstanding in the work of the Lord.

1 Corinthians 15:58

283.

Give an offering according to the extent that God has blessed you.

1 Corinthians 16:2

284.

Stay alert, stand firm in the faith, show courage, be strong.

1 Corinthians 16:13

285.

Everything you do should be done in love.

1 Corinthians 16:14

286.

Do not acknowledge anyone from an outward human point of view.

2 Corinthians 5:16

287.
Do not become partners with those who do not believe.
2 Corinthians 6:14

288.
Come out from among them and be separate.
2 Corinthians 6:17

289.
Sow generously. give as you have decided in your heart.
2 Corinthians 9:6

290.
Do note wage war according to human standards.
2 Corinthians 10:3

291.
The one who boasts must boast in the Lord.
2 Corinthians 10:17

292.
Examine yourself to see if you are in the faith.
2 Corinthians 13:12

293.
Remember the poor.
Galatians 2:10

294.
Throw out the slave woman and her son.
Galatians 4:30

295.
Do not be subject again to the yoke of slavery.
Galatians 5:1

296.
Do not use your freedom as an opportunity to indulge your flesh.
Galatians 5:13

297.
Love your neighbour as yourself.
Galatians 5:14

298.
Live by the Spirit and you will not carry out the desires of the flesh.
Galatians 5:16

299.
You cannot do what you want.
Galatians 5:17

300.
Do not be conceited.
Galatians 5:25

301.
Carry one another's burden.
Galatians 6:2

302.
Do not grow weary doing good. Do good to all people.
Galatians 6:9-10

303.
Approach God with boldness and confidence.
Ephesians 3:12

304.
Live worthy of the calling with which you have been called.
Ephesians 4:1

305.
Be humble, gentle, patient, bear one another in love.
Ephesians 4:2

306.
Make every effort to keep the unity of the spirit in the bond of peace.
Ephesians 4:3

307.
Practice the truth in love
Ephesians 4:15

308.
Lay aside the old man.
Ephesians 4:22

309.
Be renewed in the spirit of your mind.
Ephesians 4:23

310.
Put on the new man who has been created in God's image.
Ephesians 4:24

311.
Speak the truth with your neighbour.
Ephesians 4:25

312.
Be angry and do not sin.
Ephesians 4:26

313.
Do not let the sun go down on the cause of your anger.
Ephesians 4:26

314.
Do not give the devil and opportunity.
Ephesians 4:27

315.
Labour with your own hands.
Ephesians 4:28

316.
Share with the one who has need.
Ephesians 4:28

317.
Let no unwholesome word come from your mouth, but only what is beneficial for the building up of the one in need.
Ephesians 4:29

318.
Do not grieve the holy Spirit of God.
Ephesians 4:30

319.
Put away every kind of bitterness, anger, wrath, quarrelling, and evil slanderous talk.
Ephesians 4:31

320.
Be kind one to another, compassionate, forgiving.
Ephesians 4:32

321.
Present your bodies as a sacrifice, alive, holy and pleasing to God.
Romans 12:1

322.

Do not be conformed to this present world.

Romans 12:2

323.

Be transformed by the renewing of your mind.

Romans 12:2

324.

Be imitators of God.

Ephesians 5:2

325.

Live in love.

Ephesians 5:2

326.

Do not engage in sexual immorality, impurity of any kind or greed.

Ephesians 5:3

327.

There should be no vulgar speech, foolish talk, or coarse jesting (all of which are out of character)

Ephesians 5:4

328.

Give thanks.

Ephesians 5:4

329.
Do not be deceived with empty words.
Ephesians 5:6

330.
Do not be partakers with the sons of disobedience.
Ephesians 5:6-7

331.
Walk as children of the light.
Ephesians 5:8

332.
Do not participate in the unfruitful deeds of darkness, but rather expose them.
Ephesians 5:11

333.
Be careful how you live- not as unwise but as wise.
Ephesians 5:15

334.
Take advantage of every opportunity.
Ephesians 5:16

335.
Do not be foolish, but be wise by understanding what the Lord's will is.
Ephesians 5:17

336.
Do not get drunk with wine, which is debauchery.
Ephesians 5:18

337.
Be filled by the Spirit.
Ephesians 5:18

338.
Speak to one another in Psalms, hymns, spiritual song, singing and making music in your hearts to the Lord.
Ephesians 5:19

339.
Always give thanks to God the Father for each other in the name of our Lord Jesus Christ.
Ephesians 5:20

340.
Submit to one another out of reverence for Christ in everything.
Ephesians 5:21

341.
Wives, submit to your husbands as to the Lord.
Ephesians 5:22 see also 5:24

342.
Husbands, love your wives (as your own bodies), just as Christ loved the church and gave himself for her.
Ephesians 5:25 see also 5:28-5:33

343.
A man must leave father and mother and be joined to his wife.
Ephesians 5:31

344.
Wives must respect her husband.
Ephesians 5:33

345.
Children obey your parents in the Lord.
Ephesians 6:1

346.
Honour your father and mother, which is accompanied by a promise 'it may be well with you and you will live a long time on earth'.
Ephesians 6:2-3

347.
Fathers do not provoke your children to anger, but raise them up in the discipline and instruction of the Lord.
Ephesians 6:4

348.
Slaves obey your human masters with fear and trembling, in sincerity of your heart as to Christ.
Ephesians 6:5

349.
Do not be like those who only work when someone is watching as people pleasers.
Ephesians 6:6

350.
Obey with enthusiasm, as though serving the Lord and not people.
Ephesians 6:7

351.
Be strengthened in the Lord and in the strength of his power.
Ephesians 6:10

352.
Clothe yourself with the full armor of God.
Ephesians 6:11

353.
Do not fight against flesh and blood.
Ephesians 6:12

354.
Take up the full armor of God.
Ephesians 6:13

355.
Stand.
Ephesians 6:13

356.

Stand firm.

Ephesians 6:14

357.

Fasten the belt of truth around your waist.

Ephesians 6:14

358.

Put on the breastplate of righteousness

Ephesians 6:14

359.

Fit your feet with the preparation that comes from the good news of peace.

Ephesians 6:15

360.

Take up the shield of faith.

Ephesians 6:16

361.

Take the helmet of salvation and the sword of the spirit.

Ephesians 6:17

362.

Pray at all times in the spirit, be alert.

Ephesians 6:18

363.
Persevere in prayer for all saints.
Ephesians 6:18

364.
Speak the word fearlessly.
Philippians 1:14

365.
Conduct yourselves in a manner worthy of the gospel of Christ.
Philippians 1:27

366.
Stand firm in one spirit, in one mind, contending side by side for the faith of the gospel.
Philippians 1:27

367.
Be of the same mind, have the same love, be united in spirit, have one purpose.
Philippians 2:2

368.
Do not be motivated by selfish ambition or vanity.
Philippians 2:3

369.
Treat one another as more important than yourself.
Philippians 2:3

370.

Do not be concerned only with your interest, but the interest of others.

Philippians 2:3

371.

Have the same attitude that Christ Jesus had.

Philippians 2:5

372.

Work out your salvation with awe and reverence.

Philippians 2:12

373.

Do everything without grumbling or arguing.

Philippians 2:14

374.

Hold on to the word of life.

Philippians 2:16

375.

Be glad and rejoice.

Philippians 2:18

376.

Rejoice in the Lord.

Philippians 3:1

377.
Beware of dogs, evil workers, those who mutilate the flesh.
Philippians 3:2

378.
Worship by the spirit of God, exult in Christ Jesus, do not rely on human credentials.
Philippians 3:3

379.
Be single-minded, forgetting the things that are behind and reach out for the things that are ahead.
Philippians 3:13

380.
Strive toward the prize of the upward call of God in Christ Jesus.
Philippians 3:14

381.
Rejoice in the Lord always and again I say rejoice.
Philippians 4:4

382.
Let everyone see your gentleness.
Philippians 4:5

383.
Do not be anxious about anything, instead in every situation, tell your requests to God.
Philippians 4:6

384.
Whatever is true, whatever is worthy of respect, whatever is just, whatever is pure, whatever is commendable, if something is excellent or praiseworthy, think about these things.
Philippians 4:8

385.
Be content in any circumstance.
Philippians 4:11

386.
Live worthily of the Lord and please him in all respects bearing fruit in every good deed, growing in the knowledge of God.
Colossians 1:10

387.
Remain in the faith, established and firm, without shifting from the hope of the gospel that you heard.
Colossians 1:23

388.
Be careful not to allow anyone to captivate you through an empty, deceitful philosophy that is according to human traditions and the elemental spirits of the world, and not according to Christ.
Colossians 2:8

389.
Do not let anyone judge you with respect to food or drink, or in the matter of a feast, new moon or Sabbath days.
Colossians 2:16

390.
Seek the things above, where Christ is, seated at the right hand of God.
Colossians 3:1

391.
Keep thinking about things above, not things on the earth.
Colossians 3:2

392.
Put to death whatever in your nature belongs to the earth sexual immorality, impurity, shameful passion, evil desire, and greed which is idolatry.
Colossians 3:5

393.
Put off all such things as anger, rage, malice, slander, abusive language from your mouth.
Colossians 3:8

394.
Do not lie to one another.
Colossians 3:9

395.
Clothe yourself with a heart of mercy, kindness, humility, gentleness, and patience.
Colossians 3:12

396.
Bear with one another and forgive one another.
Colossians 3:13

397.
Let the peace of Christ be in control in your heart and be thankful.
Colossians 3:15

398.
Let the word of Christ dwell in you richly, teaching and exhorting one another with all wisdom, singing Psalms, hymns and spiritual songs, all with grace in your hearts to God.
Colossians 3:16

399.
Whatever you do in word or deed, do it all in the name of the Lord Jesus, giving thanks to God the father through him.
Colossians 3:17

400.
Wives, submit to your husbands, s is fitting in the Lord.
Colossians 3:18

401.
Husbands love your wives and do not be embittered against them.
Colossians 3:19

402.
Children, obey your parents in everything, for this is pleasing to the Lord.
Colossians 3:20

403.
Father, do not provoke your children, so they will not become disheartened.
Colossians 3:1

404.
Slaves, obey your earthly master in every respect, not only when they are watching- like those who are strictly people-pleasers- but with a sincere heart pleasing the Lord.
Colossians 3:22

405.
Whatever you do, work at it with enthusiasm, as to the Lord and not for people.
Colossians 3:23 reason vs. 24

406.
Master, treat your slaves with justice and fairness, because you know that you also have a master in heaven.
Colossians 4:1

407.
Be devoted to prayer, keeping alert in it with thanksgiving.
Colossians 4:2

408.
Conduct yourself with wisdom toward outsiders making the most of the opportunities.
Colossians 4:5

409.
Let your speech always be gracious, seasoned with salt, so that you may know how you should answer everyone.
Colossians 4:6

410.
Give in a ways worthy of God who call you to his own kingdom and his glory
1 Thessalonians 2:12

411.
Possess your own body in holiness and honor.
1 Thessalonians 4:4

412.
Do not violate the right of your brother or take advantage of him.
1 Thessalonians 4:6

413.
Love one another.
1 Thessalonians 4:9

414.

Aspire to lead a quiet life to attend to your own business, and to work with your hands.

1 Thessalonians 4:11

415.

Do not grieve like those who have no hope.

1 Thessalonians 4:13

416.

We must not sleep as the rest, but must stay alert and sober.

1 Thessalonians 5:6

417.

Stay sober by putting on the breastplate of faith and love and as a helmet our hope for salvation.

1 Thessalonians 5:8

418.

Encourage one another, and build up each other.

1 Thessalonians 5:11

419.

Acknowledge those who labour among you and preside over you in the Lord and admonish you, and esteem them most highly in love because of their work

1 Thessalonians 5:13

420.
Admonish the undisciplined, comfort the discouraged, help the weak, be patient toward all.
1 Thessalonians 5:14

421.
Do not pay back evil for evil to anyone, but always pursue what is good for one another and for all.
1 Thessalonians 5:15

422.
Always rejoice.
1 Thessalonians 5:16

423.
Constantly pray.
1 Thessalonians 5:17

424.
In everything give thanks, for this is God's will for you in Christ Jesus.
1 Thessalonians 5:18

425.
Do not extinguish the Spirit.
1 Thessalonians 5:19

426.
Do not treat prophecies with contempt.
1 Thessalonians 5:20

427.
Examine all things, hold fast to what is good.
1 Thessalonians 5:21

428.
Stay away from every form of evil.
1 Thessalonians 5:22

429.
have this letter read to all the brothers and sisters
1 Thessalonians 5:27

430.
Keep away from any brother who lives an undisciplined life.
2 Thessalonians 3:6

431.
Work quietly and provide your own food to eat.
2 Thessalonians 3:12

432.
Do not grow weary doing what is right.
2 Thessalonians 3:13

433.
Do not spread false teachings, or occupy yourself with myths and interminable genealogies.
1 Timothy 1:3

434.
hold firmly to faith and a good conscience.
1 Timothy 1:19

435.
Requests, prayers, intercessions, and thanks should be offered on behalf of all people, even for kings and all who are in authority, that we may lead a peaceful and quiet life in all Godliness and dignity.
1 Timothy 2:1-2

436.
Men should pray in every place, lifting up holy hands without anger or dispute.
1 Timothy 2:8

437.
Women are to dress in suitable apparel, with modesty and self-control.
1 Timothy 2:9

438.
Women must learn quietly with all submissiveness.
1 Timothy 2:11

439.
Reject those myths fit only for the Godless and gullible, and train yourself for Godliness.
1 Timothy 4:7

440.
Exercise.
1 Timothy 4:8

441.
Set an example for the believers in your speech, conduct, love, faithfulness, and purity.
1 Timothy 4:12

442.
Give attention to the public reading of scripture, to exhortation, to teaching.
1 Timothy 4:13

443.
Do not neglect the spiritual gift you have.
1 Timothy 4:14

444.
Be conscientious about how you live and what you teach persevere in this, because by doing so you will save both yourself and those who listen to you.
1 Timothy 4:16

445.
Do not address an older man harshly but appeal to him as a father.
1 Timothy 5:1

446.
Speak to younger men as brothers, older women as mothers, younger women as sisters with complete purity.
1 Timothy 5:1-2

447.
Honor widows who are truly in need.
1 Timothy 5:3

448.
Don't be lazy, a gossiper or busy bodied.
1 Timothy 5:13

449.
Elders who provide effective leadership must be counted worthy of double honor, especially those who work hard in speaking and teaching.
1 Timothy 5:17

450.
Do not accept an accusation against an elder unless it can be confirmed by two or three witnesses.
1 Timothy 5:19

451.
Those guilty of sin must be rebuked before all, as a warning to the rest.
1 Timothy 5:20

452.
Do not lay hands on anyone hastily and so identify with the sins of others. Keep yourself pure.
1 Timothy 5:22

453.
Stop drinking just water, but use a little wine for your digestion and for your frequent illnesses.
1 Timothy 5:23

454.
Do not love money.
1 Timothy 6:10

455.
Pursue righteousness, Godliness, faithfulness, love, endurance and gentleness.
1 Timothy 6:11

456.
Compete well for the faith and lay hold of that eternal life you were called for and made your confession for I the presence of many witnesses.
1 Timothy 6:12

457.
Those who are rich, in this world's goods, do not be haughty or set your hope on riches, which are uncertain, but on God who richly provides us with all things for our enjoyment. Do good, be rich in good deeds. Be generous givers, share with others.
1 Timothy 6:17-18 reason vs. 19

458.
Avoid the profane chatter and absurdities of so-called 'knowledge'.
1 Timothy 6:20

459.
Be strong in the grace that is in Christ Jesus.
2 Timothy 2:1

460.
Take your share of suffering as a good soldier of Christ Jesus.
2 Timothy 2:3

461.
Do not get entangled in matters of everyday life.
2 Timothy 2:4 reason vs. 4

462.
Endure all things for the sake of those chosen by God.
2 Timothy 2:10 reason vs. 10

463.
Do not wrangle over words. This is of no benefit, it just brings ruin on those who listen.
2 Timothy 2:14

464.
Make every effort to present yourself before God as a proven worker who does not need to be ashamed, teaching the messenger of truth accurately.
2 Timothy 2:15

465.
Avoid profane chatter.
2 Timothy 2:16

466.
Keep away from youthful passions.
2 Timothy 2:22

467.
Pursue righteousness, faithfulness, love and peace in company with others who call on the Lord from a pure heart.
2 Timothy 2:22

468.
Reject foolish and ignorant controversies.
2 Timothy 2:23

469.
Do not engage in heated disputes.
2 Timothy 2:24

470.
Be kind toward all, an apt teacher, patient, correcting opponents with gentleness.
2 Timothy 2:24-25

471.
Do not be lovers of yourselves, lovers of money, boastful, arrogant, blasphemers, disobedient to parents, ungrateful, unholy, unloving, irreconcilable slanderers, without self- control, savage, opposed to what is good, treacherous, reckless, conceited, loving pleasure rather than loving God.
2 Timothy 3:2-4

472.
Preach the message, be ready whether it is convenient or not, reprove, rebuke, exhort with complete patience and instruction.
2 Timothy 4:2

473.
Be controlled in all things, endure hardship, do an evangelist's work, fulfil your ministry.
2 Timothy 4:5

474.
Complete well, finish the race, keep the faith.
2 Timothy 4:7

475.
Older men are to be temperate, dignified, self- controlled, sound in faith, in love, and in endurance.
Titus 2:2

476.
Older women should train younger women to love their husband, children, to be self-controlled, pure, fulfilling their duties at home, kind, being subject to their own husbands.
Titus 2:3-5

477.
Younger men should be self-controlled.
Titus 2:6

478.
Reject Godless ways and worldly lives.
Titus 2:12

479.
Don't let anyone look down on you.
Titus 2:15

480.
Be subject to rulers and authorities, be obedient.
Titus 3:1

481.
Do not slander anyone, be peaceable, gently showing complete courtesy to all people.
Titus 3:2

482.
Avoid foolish controversies, genealogies, quarrels, and fights about the law, because they are useless and empty.
Titus 3:9

483.
Reject a divisive person after one or two warnings.
Titus 3:10 reason vs. 11

484.
See to it, brothers and sisters, that none of you has an evil, unbelieving heart that forsakes the living God.
Hebrews 3:12

485.
Exhort one another each day, as long as it is called 'Today' that none of you may become hardened by sin's deception.
Hebrews 3:13

486.
Do not harden your hearts as in rebellion.
Hebrews 3:8 and 3:25

487.
Listen as he speaks.
Hebrews 4:7

488.
Confidently approach the throne of grace to receive mercy and find grace whenever we need help.
Hebrews 4:16

489.
Offer both request and supplications, with loud cries and tears, to the one who is able to save you from death.
Hebrews 5:7

490.
Progress beyond the elementary instructions about Christ and move on to maturity.
Hebrews 6:1

491.
Do not be sluggish, but imitators of those who through faith and perseverance inherit the promises.
Hebrews 6:12

492.
Hold unwaveringly to the hope that we confess, for the one who made the promise is trustworthy.
Hebrews 10:23

493.
Spur one another on to love and good works.
Hebrews 10:24

494.
Do not forsake the assembly of yourselves together.
Hebrews 10:25

495.
Do not deliberately keep sinning after receiving the knowledge of the truth.
Hebrews 10:26

496.
Do not throw away your confidence, because it is a great reward.
Hebrews 10:35

497.
Live by faith.
Hebrews 10:38

498.
Aspire to a better land, a heavenly one.
Hebrews 11:16

499.
Get rid of every weight and the sin that clings so closely, and run with endurance the race set out for us.
Hebrews 12:1

500.
Keep your eyes fixed on Jesus, the pioneer and perfecter of your faith.
Hebrews 12:2

501.
Think of him who endured such opposition against himself by sinners, so that you may not grow weary in your souls and give up.
Hebrews 12:3

502.
Do not scorn the Lord's discipline or give up when he corrects you.
Hebrews 12:5

503.
Endure your suffering and discipline.
Hebrews 12:7

504.
Pursue peace with everyone, and holiness.
Hebrews 12:14

505.
Since we are receiving an unshakable kingdom let us give thanks, and through this let us offer worship pleasing to God in devotion and awe.
Hebrews 12:28

506.
Do not neglect hospitality, because through it some have entertained angels without knowing it.
Hebrews 13:2

507.
Remember those in prison, and those ill-treated.
Hebrews 13:3

508.
Marriage must be honoured among all and the marriage bed kept undefiled.
Hebrews 13:4

509.
Your conduct must be free from the love of money and you must be content with what you have.
Hebrews 13:5

510.
Remember your leaders.
Hebrews 13:7

511.
Do not be carried away by all sort of strange teachings.
Hebrews 13:9

512.
Continually offer up a sacrifice of praise to God, that is, the fruit of our lips, acknowledging his name.
Hebrews 13:15

513.

Do not neglect to do good and to share what you have, for God is pleased with such sacrifices.

Hebrews 13:16

514.

Obey your leaders and submit to them.

Hebrews 13:17

515.

Consider it nothing but joy when you fall into all sorts of trials.

James 1:2

516.

Endure testing.

James 1:12

517.

Do not say when you are tempted 'I am tempted by God.'

James 1:13

518.

Do not be led astray.

James 1:16

519.

Be quick to listen, slow to speak, slow to anger.

James 1:19

520.
Put away all filth and evil excess and humbly welcome the message implanted within you, which is able to save your souls.
James 1:21

521.
Be sure you live out the message and do not merely listen to it.
James 1:22

522.
Bridle your tongue.
James 1:26

523.
Care for orphans and widows in their misfortune and keep yourself unstained by the world.
James 1:27

524.
Do not show prejudice if you possess faith in our glorious Lord Jesus Christ.
James 2:1

525.
Do not make distinctions among yourselves and become judges with evil motives.
James 2:4

526.
Do not dishonor the poor.
James 2:6

527.
Love your neighbour as yourself.
James 2:8

528.
Speak and act as those who will be judged by a law that gives freedom.
James 2:12

529.
Do not curse people. They are made in God's image.
James 3:9

530.
Do not boast and tell lies against the truth.
James 3:14

531.
Do not be a friend with the world.
James 4:4

532.
Submit to God, resist the devil and he will flee from you.
James 4:7

533.

Draw near to God and he will draw near to you.

James 4:8

534.

humble yourself before the Lord and he will exalt you.

James 4:10

535.

Do not speak against are another, brother and sisters.

James 4:11

536.

Be patient, brother and sister, until the Lord's return.

James5:7

537.

Do not grumble against one another.

James 5:9

538.

Do not swear, let your yes be yes, and your no be no.

James 5:12

539.

Pray if you are suffering.

James 5:13

540.

Sing praises if you are in good spirits.

James 5:13

541.

Let the elders pray for you and anoint you with oil, if you are sick.

James 5:14

542.

Confess your sins to one another and pray for one another so that you may be healed.

James 5:16

543.

Get your minds ready for action by being fully sober, and set your hope completely on the grace that will be brought to you when Jesus Christ is revealed.

1 Peter 1:13

544.

Do not comply with the evil urges you used to follow in your arrogance.

1 Peter 1:14

545.

Become holy yourself in all of your conduct.

1 Peter 1:15

546.
Live out the time of your temporary residence, live in reverence
1 Peter 1:17

547.
Love one another earnestly from a pure heart
1 Peter 1:22

548.
Get rid of all evil and all deceit and hypocrisy and envy and all slander.
1 Peter 2:1

549.
Yearn like newborn infants for pure, spiritual milk, so that by it you may grow up to salvation.
1 Peter 2:2

550.
Keep away from fleshly desires that do battle against the soul.
1 Peter 2:11

551.
Maintain good conduct among the non-Christians, so that though they now malign you as wrongdoers, they may see your good deeds and glorify God when he appears.
1 Peter 2:12

552.
Be subject to every human institution for the Lord's sake kings and governors.
1 Peter 2:13-14

553.
Silence the ignorance of foolish people by doing good.
1 Peter 2:15

554.
Live as free people, not using your freedom as a pretext for evil but as God's slave.
1 Peter 2:16

555.
honor all people, love the family of believers, fear God, honor the King.
1 Peter 2:17

556.
Wives, be subject to your own husbands.
1 Peter 3:1

557.
Let your beauty not be external, the braiding of hair and wearing lot of gold jewelry or fine clothes, but the inner person of the heart, the lasting beauty of a gentle and tranquil spirit which precious in God's sight
1 Peter 3:3-4

558.
Husbands, treat your wives with consideration as the weaker partners and show them honor as fellow heirs of the grace of life. In this way nothing will hinder your prayers.
1 Peter 3:7

559.
Be harmonious, sympathetic, affectionate, compassionate and humble.
1 Peter 3:8

560.
Do not return evil for evil or insult for insult, but instead bless others because you were called to inherit a blessing.
1 Peter 3:9

561.
Keep your tongue from evil, and your lips from uttering deceit.
1 Peter 3:10

562.
Turn away from evil and do good; seek peace and pursue it.
1 Peter 3:11

563.
Set Christ apart as Lord in your hearts and always be ready to give an answer to anyone who asks about the hope you possess. Do it with courtesy and respect, keeping a good conscience, so that those who slander your good conduct in Christ may be put to shame when they accuse you.
Peter 3:15-16

564.
Spend the rest of your time on earth concerned about the will of God and not human desires.
1 Peter 4:2

565.

Be willing to suffer in the flesh.

1 Peter 4:1

566.

Be self-controlled and sober-minded for the sake of prayer.

1 Peter 4:7

567.

Keep your love for one another fervent, because love covers a multitude of sin.

1 Peter 4:8

568.

Show hospitality to one another without complaining.

1 Peter 4:9

569.

Use your gift to serve one another as good stewards of the varied grace of God.

1 Peter 4:10

570.

Speak with God's words. Serve in the strength that God supplies.

1 Peter 4:11

571.
Elders, give a shepherd's care to God's flock among you, exercising oversight not merely as duty but willingly under God's direction, not for shameful profit but eagerly and do not hold it over those entrusted to you but be examples to the flock.
1Peter 5:3

572.
Young men, be subject to the elders.
1 Peter 5:5

573.
Clothe yourselves with humility toward one another.
1 Peter 5:5

574.
Cast your care on him because he cares for you.
1 Peter 5:7

575.
Be sober and alert. Your enemy the devil, like a roaring lion, is on the prowl looking for someone to devour.
1 Peter 5:8

576.
Resist the devil.
1 Peter 5:9

577.
Make every effort to add to your faith excellence, to excellence, knowledge to knowledge, self-control to self-control, perseverance to perseverance, Godliness to Godliness, brotherly affection to brotherly affection, unselfish love.
2 Peter 1:5-7 reason vs. 8

578.
Make every effort to be sure of your calling and election.
2 Peter 1:10 reason vs. 6

579.
Do not indulge your fleshly desires, or despise authority.
2 Peter 2:10

580.
Strive to be found at peace, without spot or blemish, when you come into his presence.
2 Peter 3:14

581.
Walk in the light.
1 John 1:7

582.
Keep his commandments.
1 John 2:3

583.

Walked just as Jesus walked.

1 John 2:6

584.

Do not love the world or the things in the world.

1 John 2:15

585.

Remain in him.

1 John 2:28

586.

Practice righteousness.

1 John 2:29 see 3:7

587.

Do not practice sin.

1 John 3:4

588.

Love one another.

1 John 3:11 see also 2 John 1:5

589.

Love your fellow Christians.

1 John 3:14

590.

Let us not love with word or with tongue but indeed truth.

1 John 3:18

591.

Keep his commandments and do the things that are pleasing to him.

1 John 3:22

592.

Believe in the name of Jesus Christ, and love one another.

1 John 3:23

593.

Do not believe every spirit, but test the spirits to determine if they are from God.

1 John 4:1

594.

Love one another.

1 John 4:7

595.

Live through Christ.

1 John 4:9

596.

Guard yourselves from idols.

1 John 5:21

597.
Live according to the truth.
2 John 1:4

598.
Remain in the teachings of Christ.
2 John 1:9-10

599.
Do not imitate what is bad but what is good.
3 John 1:11

600.
Contend earnestly for the truth.
Jude 1:3

601.
Do not travel down Cain's path or abandon yourselves to Balaam's error
Jude 1:11

602.
Build yourselves up in your most holy faith, by praying in the holy Spirit.
Jude 1:20

603.
Maintain yourselves in the love of God, while anticipating the mercy of our Lord Jesus Christ that brings eternal life.
Jude 1:21

604.
Have mercy on those who waver.
Jude 1:22

605.
Save others by snatching them out of the fire, have mercy on others, coupled with fear of God, hating even the clothes stained by the flesh.
Jude 1:23

606.
Do not be afraid.
Revelation 1:17

607.
Remain faithful, even to the point of death, and I will give you the crown that is life itself.
Revelation 2:10

608.
Hold on to what you have until I come.
Revelation 2:25

609.
Do not love your life too much that you are afraid to die.
Revelation 12:11

610.
Fear God and give him glory.
Revelation 14:7

611.
Worship the one who made heaven and earth, the sea and springs of water.
Revelation 14:7

612.
Stay alert.
Revelation 16:15

613.
Worship God.
Revelation 9:10 see also 22:9

On Worship

1.
Shout for joy.
Psalms 5:11

2.
Thank the Lord with all your heart.
Psalms 9:1

3.
Tell about your amazing deeds.
Psalms 9:1

4.
Be happy and rejoice in God.
Psalms 9:2

5.
Sing praises to God.
Psalms 9:2 see also 18:49

6.
Sing praises to the Lord.
Psalms 9:11

7.
Tell the nations what he has done.
Psalms 9:11

8.
Tell about God's praiseworthy acts.
Psalms 9:14

9.
I will rejoice because of your deliverance.
Psalms 9:14 see also 13:5

10.
Praise the Lord who guides you.
Psalms 16:7

11.
Give thanks to God before the nations.
Psalms 18:49

12.
Fear the Lord.
Psalms 19:9

13.
Let your words and thoughts be acceptable in God's sight.
Psalms 19:4

14.
Shout for joy over your victory.
Psalm 20:15

15.
Sing and praise God's power.
Psalms 21:13

16.
Offer praise in the great assembly.
Psalms 22:25

17.
Tell the next generation about the sovereign Lord.
Psalms 22:30

18.
Come before the Lord in prayer.
Psalms 25:1

19.
Offer sacrifices in his dwelling place and shout for joy.
Psalms 27:6

20.
Sing praises to the Lord.
Psalms 27:6

21.

Cry out to God for help.

Psalms 28:2

22.

Lift up your hands toward his holy temple.

Psalms 28:2

23.

Sing to the Lord in gratitude.

Psalms 28:7

24.

Sing to the Lord faithful followers, give thanks to his holy name.

Psalms 30:4

25.

Let your heart sing and not be silent. Always give thanks to God.

Psalms 30:12

26.

Be happy and rejoice in God's faithfulness.

Psalms 31:7

27.

Declare, you are my God.

Psalms 31:1

28.

Love the Lord.

Psalms 31:23

29.

Pray to God while there is a window of opportunity.

Psalms 32:6

30.

Rejoice in the Lord and be happy.

Psalms 32:11

31.

Shout for joy.

Psalms 32:11 see also 33:1

32.

Offer God praise.

Psalms 33:1

33.

Give thanks to the Lord with the harp.

Psalms 33:2

34.

Sing to him to the accompaniment of a ten- stringed instrument.

Psalms 33:2

35.

Sing to him a new song.

Psalms 33:3

36.

Play skillfully as you shout out your praises to him.

Psalms 33:3

37.

Fear the Lord, stand in awe of him.

Psalms 33:8

38.

Praise the Lord at all times, continually.

Psalms 34:1

39.

Praise his name together.

Psalms 34:3

40.

Continually give thanks to his name.

Psalms 44:8

41.

Clap your hands.

Psalms 47:1

42.

Shout out to God in celebration.

Psalms 47:1

43.

Sing to God 'sing'.

Psalms 47:6 see also 64:8, 68:32

44.

Sing a well-written song.

Psalms 47:7

45.

Be humble and repent.

Psalms 51:7

46.

give to God thank-offerings.

Psalms 56:12

47.

Praise his loyal love in the morning.

Psalms 59:16

48.

Sing praises to his name continually.

Psalms 61:8

49.

Praise him with your lips.

Psalms 63:5

50.

Pursue God.

Psalms 63:8

51.

Rejoice in the Lord, take shelter in him.

Psalms 64:10

52.

Shout out praise to God, all the earth.

Psalms 66:1

53.

Sing praises about the majesty of his reputation.

Psalms 66:2

54.

Give him the honor he deserves.

Psalms 66:2

55.

Say to God, 'how awesome are your deeds! Because of your great power your enemies cower in fear before you. All the earth worships you and gives praises to you! They sing praises to your name'.

Psalms 66:3-4

56.

Praise our God, loudly proclaim his praise.

Psalms 66:8

57.

Acknowledge God's power.

Psalms 68:34

58.

Magnify him as you give him thanks.

Psalms 69:30

59.

Speak of his splendor all day long.

Psalms 71:8

60.

Pray with hands raised.

Psalms 77:2

61.

Remember the works of the Lord.

Psalms 77:11

62.

Shout for joy to God.

Psalms 81:1

63.

Sing a song and play the tambourine, the pleasant sounding harp, and the ten- stringed instruments.

Psalms 81:2

64.

Open your mouth wide and God will fill it.

Psalms 81:10

65.

Spread out your hands in prayer.

Psalms 88:9

66.

Sing for joy.

Psalms 95:1

67.

Shout out praises.

Psalms 95:1

68.

Enter his presence with thanksgiving.

Psalms 95:2

69.

Shout out to him in celebration.

Psalms 95:2

70.

Bow down and worship.

Psalms 95:6

71.

Kneel before the Lord.

Psalms 95:6

72.

Sing to the Lord a new song.

Psalms 96:1

73.

Sing to the Lord! Praise his name.

Psalms 92:2

74.

Announce every day how he delivers.

Psalms 96:2

75.

Bring an offering and enter his courts.

Psalms 96:8

76.

Worship the Lord in holy attire!

Psalms 96:9

77.

Tremble before him.

Psalms 96:9

78.

Say 'The Lord reigns.

Psalms 96:10

79.

Rejoice in the Lord.

Psalms 97:12

80.

Give thanks to his holy name.

Psalms 97:12

81.

Shout out praises to the Lord.

Psalms 97:12

82.

Break out in a joyful shout and sing.

Psalms 98:4

83.

Sing to the Lord accompanied by a harp and the sound of music.

Psalms 98:5

84.

With trumpets and the blaring of the ram's horn, shout out praises before the king, the Lord.

Psalms 98:6

85.

Praise his great and awesome name.

Psalms 99:3

86.

Praise the Lord our God. Worship before his footstool.

Psalms 99:5

87.

Shout praises to the Lord.

Psalms 100:1

88.

Worship the Lord with Joy.

Psalms 100:2

89.

Enter his presence with joyful singing.

Psalms 100: 2

90.

Acknowledge that the Lord is God.

Psalms 100: 3

91.

Enter his gates with thanksgiving, and his courts with praise.

Psalms 100:4

92.

Give him thanks.

Psalms 100:4

93.

Praise his name.

Psalms 100:4

94.

With all that is within you, praise his holy name.

Psalms 103:1

95.

Give thanks to the Lord.

Psalms 105:1

96.

Call on his name.

Psalms 105:1

97.

Sing to him, make music to him.

Psalms 105:2

98.

Tell about all his miraculous deeds.

Psalms 105:2

99.

Boast about his holy name.

Psalms 105:3

100.

Seek his presence continually.

Psalms 105:4

101.

Recall the miraculous deeds he performed.

Psalms 105:5

102.

Give thanks to the Lord for he is good, his loyal love endures.

Psalms 106:1

103.

Let those delivered by the Lord speak out, those whom he delivered from the power of the enemy.

Psalms 107:2

104.

Exalt him in the assembly of the people.

Psalms 107:32

105.
Thank the Lord profusely. Praise him in the middle of a crowd.
Psalms 109:30

106.
Be generous to the needy.
Psalms 112:9

107.
Applaud him.
Psalms 117:1

108.
Pray for the peace of Jerusalem.
Psalms 122:6

109.
Laugh loudly and shout for joy.
Psalms 126:2

110.
Lift your hands toward the sanctuary and praise the Lord.
Psalms 134:2

111.
Bow down towards his holy temple.
Psalms 138:2

112.
Live in his presence.
Psalms 140:13

113.
Sing a new song accompanied by ten-stringed instruments.
Psalms 144:9

114.
Praise him every day.
Psalms 145:2

115.
Praise him continually.
Psalms 145:2

116.
Praise the Lord with your mouth.
Psalms 145:21

117.
Offer to the Lord a song of thanks.
Psalms 147:7

118.
Sing to the Lord a new song.
Psalms 149:1

119.

Praise him in the assembly of the Godly.

Psalms 149:1

120.

Praise his name with dancing.

Psalms 149:3

121.

Praise him with the blast of the horn.

Psalms 150:3

122.

Praise him with the lyre and the harp.

Psalms 150:3

123.

Praise him with the tambourine and with dancing.

Psalms 150:4

124.

Praise him with stringed instruments and the flute.

Psalms 150:4

125.

Praise him with loud cymbals.

Psalms 150:5

126.

Praise him with clanging cymbals.

Psalms 150:5

127.

Let everything that has breath praise the Lord.

Psalms 150: 6

www.ingramcontent.com/pod-product-compliance
Lightning Source LLC
Chambersburg PA
CBHW071459070526
44578CB00001B/393